Christmas Songs

illustrated by TRICIA HARRISON

Ladybird Books

Have yourself a merry little Christmas

Have yourself a merry little Christmas,
   let your heart be light,
From now on, our troubles will be out of sight.

Have yourself a merry little Christmas,
   make the yule-tide gay,
From now on, our troubles will be miles away.

Here we are as in olden days,
  happy golden days of yore,
Faithful friends who are dear to us
  gather near to us once more.
Through the years we all will be together,
  if the fates allow,
Hang a shining star upon the highest bough,
And have yourself a merry little Christmas now.

5

Jingle bells

Dashing through the snow
In a one-horse open sleigh,
O'er the fields we go,
Laughing all the way.
Bells on bob-tail ring,
Making spirits bright.
What fun it is to ride and sing
 a sleighing song tonight.

Jingle bells, jingle bells,
 jingle all the way.
Oh, what fun it is to ride
 in a one-horse open sleigh.
Jingle bells, jingle bells,
 jingle all the way.
Oh, what fun it is to ride
 in a one-horse open sleigh.

Now the ground is white
Go it while you're young.
Take the girls tonight,
Sing this sleighing song.
Get a bob-tailed bay,
Two-forty for his speed.
Then hitch him to an open sleigh
And you will take the lead.

Santa Claus is comin' to town

You better watch out, you better not cry,
Better not pout, I'm telling you why:
Santa Claus is comin' to town.

He's making a list and checking it twice,
Gonna find out who's naughty and nice:
Santa Claus is comin' to town.

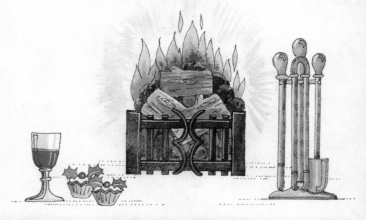

He sees you when you're sleepin',
He knows when you're awake,
He knows if you've been bad or good,
So be good for goodness sake.

You better watch out, you better not cry,
Better not pout, I'm telling you why,
Santa Claus is comin' to town.

Rockin' around the Christmas tree

Rockin' around the Christmas tree
  at the Christmas party hop.
Mistletoe hung where you can see
  ev'ry couple tries to stop.

You will get a sentimental feeling
  when you hear
Voices singing, "Let's be jolly,
  Deck the halls with boughs of holly."
Rockin' around the Christmas tree.
Have a happy holiday.
Ev'ryone dancing merrily
  in the new old fashioned way.

Rockin' around the Christmas tree
  let the Christmas spirit ring.
Later we'll have some pumpkin pie
  and we'll do some carolling.

You will get a sentimental feeling
  when you hear
Voices singing, "Let's be jolly,
  Deck the halls with boughs of holly."
Rockin' around the Christmas tree.
Have a happy holiday.
Ev'ryone dancing merrily
  in the new old fashioned way.

Let it snow!
Let it snow! Let it snow!

Oh the weather outside is frightful
But the fire is so delightful,
And since we've no place to go,
Let it snow!
Let it snow!
Let it snow!

It doesn't show signs of stopping
And I brought some corn for popping,
The lights are turned way down low,
Let it snow!
Let it snow!
Let it snow!

When we finally kiss goodnight,
How I'll hate going out in the storm!
But if you'll really hold me tight,
All the way home I'll be warm.

The fire is slowly dying
And my dear we're still goodbyeing,
But as long as you love me so,
Let it snow!
Let it snow!
Let it snow!

Rudolph the red-nosed reindeer

You know Dasher and Dancer and Prancer
   and Vixen,
Comet and Cupid and Donner and Blitzen,
But do you recall the most famous reindeer
   of all?

Rudolph the red-nosed reindeer
   had a very shiny nose,
And if you ever saw it,
   you would even say it glows.

All of the other reindeer
    used to laugh and call him names,
They never let poor Rudolph
    join in any reindeer games.
Then one foggy Christmas eve,
    Santa came to say,
"Rudolph, with your nose so bright,
    won't you guide my sleigh tonight?"
Then how the reindeer loved him
    as they shouted out with glee:
"Rudolph the red-nosed reindeer,
    you'll go down in history!"

15

We wish you a merry Christmas

We wish you a merry Christmas,
We wish you a merry Christmas,
We wish you a merry Christmas
and a happy New Year!

Good tidings we bring
For you and your kin.
We wish you a merry Christmas
and a happy New Year!

Now bring us some figgy pudding,
Now bring us some figgy pudding,
Now bring us some figgy pudding,
Now bring some to us here.

We won't go until we get it,
We won't go until we get it,
We won't go until we get it,
So bring some right here.

We all like our figgy pudding,
We all like our figgy pudding,
So bring us some figgy pudding,
With all its good cheer!

We wish you a merry Christmas,
We wish you a merry Christmas,
We wish you a merry Christmas
  and a happy New Year!

17

Winter wonderland

Sleigh bells ring, are you list'nin'?
In the lane snow is glist'nin',
A beautiful sight,
We're happy tonight,
Walkin' in a winter wonderland!

Gone away is the bluebird,
Here to stay is a new bird,
He sings a love song,
As we go along,
Walkin' in a winter wonderland!

In the meadow we can build a snowman,
Then pretend that he is Parson Brown.
He'll say, "Are you married?"
We'll say, "No, man!
But you can do the job when you're in town!"

Later on we'll conspire
As we dream by the fire
To face unafraid the plans that we made,
Walkin' in a winter wonderland!

Sleigh bells ring, are you list'nin'?
In the lane snow is glist'nin',
A beautiful sight,
We're happy tonight,
Walkin' in a winter wonderland!

Gone away is the bluebird,
Here to stay is a new bird,
He sings a love song,
As we go along,
Walkin in a winter wonderland!

In the meadow we can build a snowman,
Then pretend that he is Parson Brown.
He'll say, "Are you married?"
We'll say, "No, man!
But you can do the job when you're in town!"

Later on we'll conspire
As we dream by the fire
To face unafraid the plans that we made,
Walkin' in a winter wonderland!

I wish it could be Christmas every day

Oh when the snowman brings the snow,
Oh well he just might like to know
He's put a great big smile on somebody's face.
If you jump into your bed,
Quickly cover up your head,
Don't you lock the doors,
You know that sweet Santa Claus is on the way.

Oh I wish it could be Christmas ev'ry day.
When the kids start singing
 and the band begins to play.
Oh I wish it could be Christmas ev'ry day,
So let the bells ring out for Christmas.

I saw Mommy kissing Santa Claus

I saw Mommy kissing Santa Claus
Underneath the mistletoe last night;
She didn't see me creep down the stairs
to have a peep,
She thought that I was tucked up in
my bedroom fast asleep.
Then I saw Mommy tickle Santa Claus
Underneath his beard so snowy white;
Oh, what a laugh it would have been
If Daddy had only seen
Mommy kissing Santa Claus last night.

The twelve days of Christmas

On the first day of Christmas
my true love sent to me,
a partridge in a pear tree.

On the second day of Christmas
my true love sent to me,
two turtledoves
and a partridge in a pear tree.

On the third day of Christmas
my true love sent to me,
three French hens,
two turtledoves
and a partridge in a pear tree.

On the fourth day of Christmas
my true love sent to me,
four calling birds,
three French hens,
two turtledoves
and a partridge in a pear tree.

On the fifth day of Christmas
my true love sent to me,
five gold rings,
four calling birds,
three French hens,
two turtledoves
and a partridge in a pear tree.

On the sixth day of Christmas
my true love sent to me,
six geese a-laying,
five gold rings,
four calling birds,
three French hens,
two turtledoves
and a partridge in a pear tree.

On the seventh day of Christmas
my true love sent to me,
seven swans a-swimming,
six geese a-laying,
five gold rings,
four calling birds,
three French hens,
two turtledoves
and a partridge in a pear tree.

On the eighth day of Christmas
my true love sent to me,
eight maids a-milking,
seven swans a-swimming,
six geese a-laying,
five gold rings,
four calling birds,
three French hens,
two turtledoves
and a partridge in a pear tree.

On the ninth day of Christmas
my true love sent to me,
nine ladies dancing,
eight maids a-milking,
seven swans a-swimming,
six geese a-laying,
five gold rings,
four calling birds,
three French hens,
two turtledoves
and a partridge in a pear tree.

On the tenth day of Christmas
my true love sent to me,
ten lords a-leaping,
nine ladies dancing,
eight maids a-milking,
seven swans a-swimming,
six geese a-laying,
five gold rings,
four calling birds,
three French hens,
two turtledoves
and a partridge in a pear tree.

On the eleventh day of Christmas
my true love sent to me,
eleven pipers piping,
ten lords a-leaping,
nine ladies dancing,
eight maids a-milking,
seven swans a-swimming,
six geese a-laying,
five gold rings,
four calling birds,
three French hens,
two turtledoves
and a partridge in a pear tree.

On the twelfth day of Christmas
my true love sent to me,
twelve drummers drumming,
eleven pipers piping,
ten lords a-leaping,
nine ladies dancing,
eight maids a-milking,
seven swans a-swimming,
six geese a-laying,
five gold rings,
four calling birds,
three French hens,
two turtledoves
and a partridge in a pear tree.

The little drummer boy

Come they told me, pa-rum, pum pum pum,
A new born King to see, pa-rum, pum pum pum,
Our finest gifts we bring, pa-rum, pum pum pum,
To lay before the King, pa-rum, pum pum pum,
rum, pum pum pum, rum, pum pum pum,
So to honour Him, pa-rum, pum pum pum,
When we come.

Little Baby, pa-rum, pum pum pum,
I am a poor boy too, pa-rum, pum pum pum,
I have no gift to bring, pa-rum, pum pum pum,
That's fit to give our King, pa-rum, pum pum pum,
rum, pum pum pum, rum, pum pum pum,
Shall I play for you, pa-rum, pum pum pum,
On my drum?

Mary nodded, pa-rum, pum pum pum,
The Ox and Lamb kept time,
  pa-rum, pum pum pum,
I played my drum for Him,
  pa-rum, pum pum pum,
I played my best for Him, pa-rum, pum pum pum,
rum, pum pum pum, rum, pum pum pum,
Then He smiled at me, pa-rum, pum pum pum,
Me and my drum.

Sleigh ride

Just hear those sleigh bells jingle-ing,
   ring-ting-tingle-ing, too,
Come on, it's lovely weather
   for a sleigh ride together with you.
Outside the snow is falling
   and friends are calling "Yoo-hoo,"
Come on, it's lovely weather
   for a sleigh ride together with you.

Giddy-yap, giddy-yap, giddy-yap, let's go,
Let's look at the show,
We're riding in a wonderland of snow.
Giddy-yap, giddy-yap, giddy-yap, it's grand,
Just holding your hand,
We're gliding along with a song of a wintery
   fairy land,

Our cheeks are nice and rosy,
    and comfy cosy are we,
We're snuggled up together
    like two birds of a feather would be.
Let's take that road before us
    and sing a chorus or two,
Come on, it's lovely weather
    for a sleigh ride together with you.

The Christmas song

Chestnuts roasting on an open fire,
Jack Frost nipping at your nose,
Yule-tide carols being sung by a choir
And folks dressed up like Eskimos.
Ev'rybody knows a turkey and some mistletoe
Help to make the season bright.
Tiny tots with their eyes all aglow
Will find it hard to sleep tonight.

They know that Santa's on his way;
He's loaded lots of toys and goodies on his sleigh
And ev'ry mother's child is gonna spy
To see if reindeer really know how to fly.
And so, I'm offering this simple phrase
To kids from one to ninety two.
Altho' it's been said many times, many ways:
"Merry Christmas to you."

Snowy white snow and jingle bells

Looking thro' my window,
Oh! what a lovely sight I see.
Snowflakes falling ev'rywhere,
My, oh my, what can it be?
Ev'rything is gay;
It must be Christmas Day.

Snowy white snow and jingle bells
Oh! what a happy season.
Snowy white snow and jingle bells,
Echoing all day long.
Ev'ryone's gay, and wish you well
They have a simple reason.
Little red robins in the dell,
Singing a happy song.
Fairy lights and starry nights,
You can have your wish.
Candle glow and mistletoe;
It's time to steal a kiss.
Snowy white snow and jingle bells.
Join in the carol singing;
Wishing to you and yours and mine,
A very happy Christmas time.

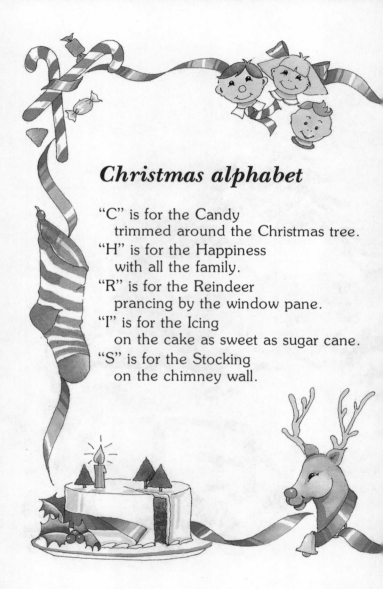

Christmas alphabet

"C" is for the Candy
   trimmed around the Christmas tree.
"H" is for the Happiness
   with all the family.
"R" is for the Reindeer
   prancing by the window pane.
"I" is for the Icing
   on the cake as sweet as sugar cane.
"S" is for the Stocking
   on the chimney wall.

"T" is for the Toys
   beneath the tree so tall.
"M" is for the Mistletoe
   where ev'ryone is kissed.
"A" is for the Angels
   who make up the Christmas list.
"S" is for old Santa
   who makes ev'ry kid his pet.
Be good and he'll bring you ev'rything
   in your CHRISTMAS ALPHABET.

39

Silver bells

Christmas makes you feel emotional.
It may bring parties or thoughts devotional.
Whatever happens or what may be,
Here is what Christmas time means to me.

City sidewalks, busy sidewalks
   dressed in holiday style.
In the air there's a feeling of Christmas.
Children laughing, people passing,
   meeting smile after smile,
And on ev'ry street corner you hear:
Silver bells, silver bells,
It's Christmas time in the city.
Ring-a-ling hear them ring,
Soon it will be Christmas Day.

Strings of streetlights, even stop lights
   blink a bright red and green,
As the shoppers rush home with their treasures.
Hear the snow crunch, see the kids bunch,
this is Santa's big scene,
And above all this bustle you hear:
Silver bells, silver bells,
It's Christmas time in the city.
Ring-a-ling hear them ring,
Soon it will be Christmas Day.

Mary's Boy Child

Long time ago in Bethlehem
* so the Holy Bible say,*
Mary's Boy Child, Jesus Christ,
* was born on Christmas Day.*

Hark, now hear the angels sing,
  a new King born today,
And Man will live for evermore,
Because of Christmas Day.
Trumpets sound and angels sing,
  listen to what they say,
That Man will live for evermore,
Because of Christmas Day.

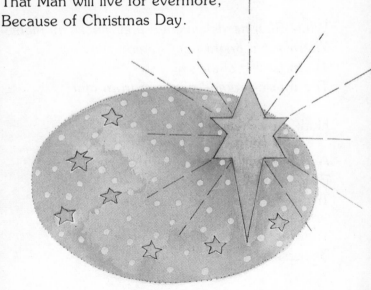

While Shepherds watched their flocks by night,
Them see a bright new shining star.
Them hear a choir sing,
The music seemed to come from afar.

Hark, now hear the angels sing,
  a new King born today,
And Man will live for evermore,
Because of Christmas Day.
Trumpets sound and angels sing,
  listen to what they say,
That Man will live for evermore,
Because of Christmas Day.

How Joseph and his wife Mary,
  come to Bethlehem that night,
Them find no place to born she Child,
Not a single room was in sight.

Hark, now hear the angels sing,
  a new King born today,
And Man will live for evermore,
Because of Christmas Day.
Trumpets sound and angels sing,
  listen to what they say,
That Man will live for evermore,
Because of Christmas Day.
Because of Christmas Day.

By and by they find a little nook
In a stable all forlorn,
And in a manger cold and dark,
Mary's little Boy was born.